90 Colon Cancer Juice and Salad Recipes:

The Comprehensive Recipe Book to Prevent and Fight Cancer

By

Joe Correa CSN

COPYRIGHT

© 2019 Live Stronger Faster Inc.

All rights reserved

Reproduction or translation of any part of this work beyond that permitted by section 107 or 108 of the 1976 United States Copyright Act without the permission of the copyright owner is unlawful.

This publication is designed to provide accurate and authoritative information in regard to the subject matter covered. It is sold with the understanding that neither the author nor the publisher is engaged in rendering medical advice. If medical advice or assistance is needed, consult with a doctor. This book is considered a guide and should not be used in any way detrimental to your health. Consult with a physician before starting this nutritional plan to make sure it's right for you.

ACKNOWLEDGEMENTS

This book is dedicated to my friends and family that have had mild or serious illnesses so that you may find a solution and make the necessary changes in your life.

90 Colon Cancer Juice and Salad Recipes:

The Comprehensive Recipe Book to Prevent and Fight Cancer

By

Joe Correa CSN

CONTENTS

Copyright

Acknowledgements

About The Author

Introduction

Commitment

90 Colon Cancer Juice and Salad Recipes: The Comprehensive Recipe Book to Prevent and Fight Cancer

Additional Titles from This Author

ABOUT THE AUTHOR

After years of Research, I honestly believe in the positive effects that proper nutrition can have over the body and mind. My knowledge and experience has helped me live healthier throughout the years and which I have shared with family and friends. The more you know about eating and drinking healthier, the sooner you will want to change your life and eating habits.

Nutrition is a key part in the process of being healthy and living longer so get started today. The first step is the most important and the most significant.

INTRODUCTION

90 Colon Cancer Juice and Salad Recipes: The Comprehensive Recipe Book to Prevent and Fight Cancer

By Joe Correa CSN

There are certain risk factors that may contribute to developing colon cancer. These factors include older age, inflammatory intestinal conditions, family history of colon cancer, sedentary lifestyle, poor diet, obesity, smoking, and alcohol.

This serious disease is the third most common cause of cancer-related deaths in the United States which is why recognizing the symptoms and changing some lifestyle habits can be a lifesaver.

Another important step you have to take in order to prevent this terrible and extremely dangerous disease is definitely a dietary lifestyle change. This life-saving decision will permanently change the way you eat, and most importantly, a healthy diet will change the way your digestive tract handles food. This means that with just a couple of simple steps, your body will start to change and you will feel much better. You will have to change the way you eat and adopt some long-term diet habits. Only this will permanently clean your digestive tract and reduce the risk of colon cancer.

But, I have to point out that in order to be 100% sure you're healthy, the diet, by itself, won't be enough. A healthy diet combined with regular exercise is the only way to successfully fight off this disease.

This unique collection of colon cancer preventing recipes will become your guide in leading a healthy life. These juices are full of fibers that will clean your entire digestive tract and wash away all the toxins you've been collecting over the years. But, that's not all, these recipes were carefully chosen to fully satisfy your taste and make you want more! They are amazingly simple to prepare. Within just a couple of minutes you will have a glass full of nutrients your body needs on a daily basis.

COMMITMENT

In order to improve my condition, I *(your name)*, commit to eating more of these foods on a daily basis and to exercise at least 30 minutes daily:

- Berries (especially blueberries), peaches, cherries, apples, apricots, oranges, lemon juice, grapefruit, tangerines, mandarins, pears, etc.
- Broccoli, spinach, collard greens, sweet potatoes, avocado, artichoke, baby corn, carrots, celery, cauliflower, onions, etc.
- Whole grains, steel-cut oats, oatmeal, quinoa, barley, etc.
- Black beans, red bean beans, garbanzo beans, lentils, etc.
- Nuts and seeds including: walnuts, cashews, flaxseeds, sesame seeds, etc.
- Fish
- 8 – 10 glasses of water

Sign here

X_____

90 COLON CANCER JUICE AND SALAD RECIPES: THE COMPREHENSIVE RECIPE BOOK TO PREVENT AND FIGHT CANCER

JUICE RECIPES

1.   Apple Ginger Juice

Ingredients:

1 large Granny Smith's apple, cored

½ cup of collard greens

1 tsp of ginger, ground

1 large cucumber

¼ cup of fresh parsley

Preparation:

Wash the apple and cut lengthwise in half. Remove the core and chop into small pieces. Set aside.

Wash the collard greens thoroughly under cold running water using a large colander. Drain and torn into small pieces. Set aside.

Wash the cucumber and cut into thin slices. Set aside.

Rinse the parsley and chop into small pieces. Set aside.

Now, combine apple, collard greens, cucumber, and parsley in a juicer and process until juiced. trans

Transfer to serving glasses and add few ice cubes.

Serve immediately.

Nutritional information per serving: Kcal: 96, Protein: 3.1g, Carbs: 28.7g, Fats: 1.2g

2. Carrot Turnip Juice

Ingredients:

2 large carrots, sliced

1 cup of turnip greens, torn

1 cup of cauliflower, chopped

1 large radish, chopped

¼ tsp of ginger, ground

2 oz of water

Preparation:

Wash and peel the carrots. Cut into thin slices and set aside.

Wash the turnip greens thoroughly under cold running water. Drain and torn into small pieces. Set aside.

Trim off the outer leaves of the cauliflower. Wash it and chop into small pieces. Fill the measuring cup and reserve the rest for later.

Wash the radish and chop into small pieces. Set aside.

Wash the radish and chop into small pieces. Set aside.

Now, combine cauliflower, carrots, radish, and turnip greens in a juicer and process until juiced. Transfer to a serving glass and stir in the ginger and water.

Add some ice and serve immediately.

Nutritional information per serving: Kcal: 75, Protein: 4.3g, Carbs: 23.3g, Fats: 0.8g

3. Lemon Grapefruit Juice

Ingredients:

2 whole lemons, peeled and halved

1 whole grapefruit, peeled and wedged

1 cup of mango, chunked

1 small Granny Smith's apple, cored

¼ tsp of ginger, ground

Preparation:

Peel the lemons and cut each lengthwise in half. Set aside.

Peel the grapefruit and divide into wedges. Cut each wedge in half and set aside.

Peel the mango and cut into chunks. Fill the measuring cup and reserve the rest for later. Set aside.

Wash the apple and cut lengthwise in half. Remove the core and cut into bite-sized pieces. Set aside.

Now, combine lemon, mango, grapefruit, and apple in a juicer and process until juiced. Transfer to a serving glass and stir in the ginger.

Add few ice cubes and serve immediately.

Enjoy!

Nutritional information per serving: Kcal: 65, Protein: 4.5g, Carbs: 16.8g, Fats: 0.8g

4. Apple Celery Juice

Ingredients:

1 small Golden Delicious apple, cored

1 cup of celery, chopped

1 cup of apricots, chopped

1 cup of strawberries, chopped

¼ tsp of cinnamon, ground

Preparation:

Wash the apple and cut lengthwise in half. Remove the core and cut into small pieces. Set aside.

Wash the celery and chop into small pieces. Set aside.

Wash the apricots and cut in half. Remove the pits and chop into small pieces. Fill the measuring cup and reserve the rest for later. Set aside.

Wash the strawberries and remove the stems. Cut into small pieces and fill the measuring cup. Reserve the rest for later.

Now, combine apple, celery, apricots, and strawberries in a juicer and process until juiced. Transfer to a serving glass and stir in the cinnamon.

Add some ice and serve immediately.

Nutritional information per serving: Kcal: 170, Protein: 4.3g, Carbs: 49.9g, Fats: 1.4g

5. Broccoli Lime Juice

Ingredients:

2 cups of broccoli, chopped

1 whole lime, peeled and halved

2 cups of kale, chopped

1 cup of cucumber, sliced

1 whole lemon, peeled and halved

1 oz of water

Preparation:

Wash the broccoli and trim off the outer leaves. Cut into small pieces and fill the measuring cup. Reserve the rest in the refrigerator.

Peel the lime and lemon. Cut each fruit lengthwise in half and set aside.

Wash the kale thoroughly under cold running water. Drain and chop into small pieces. Set aside.

Wash the cucumber and cut into thin slices. Fill the measuring cup and reserve the rest for later.

Now, combine broccoli, kale, cucumber, lime, and lemon in

a juicer and process until juiced. Transfer to a serving glass and stir in the water.

Sprinkle with some mint for some extra taste, but it's optional.

Refrigerate for 10 minutes before serving.

Enjoy!

Nutritional information per serving: Kcal: 116, Protein: 12.1g, Carbs: 34.8g, Fats: 2.2g

6. Lemon Pineapple Juice

Ingredients:

1 whole lemon, peeled

1 cup of black grapes

1 cup of pineapple, chunked

1 whole grapefruit, peeled and wedged

¼ tsp of cinnamon, ground

Preparation:

Peel the lemon and cut lengthwise in half. Set aside.

Using a sharp paring knife, cut the top of the pineapple. Gently remove all hard skin and cut into chunks. Fill the measuring cup and reserve the in the refrigerator.

Rinse the grapes thoroughly under cold running water. Remove the stems and fill the measuring cup. Set aside.

Peel the grapefruit and divide into wedges. Cut each wedge in half and set aside.

Now, combine lemon, grapes, pineapple, and grapefruit in a juicer and process until juiced. Transfer to a serving glass and stir in the cinnamon.

Add some crushed ice and serve immediately.

Nutritional information per serving: Kcal: 230, Protein: 4g, Carbs: 69.1g, Fats: 1.1g

7. Pepper Lettuce Juice

Ingredients:

1 large yellow bell pepper, chopped

1 cup of Romaine lettuce, chopped

1 cup of fennel, sliced

1 cup of cucumber, sliced

1 small zucchini, cubed

Preparation:

Wash the bell pepper and cut lengthwise in half. Remove the stem and seeds. Cut into small pieces and set aside.

Wash the Romaine lettuce thoroughly under cold running water. Drain and chop into small pieces. Set aside.

Trim off the fennel bulb and remove the green parts. Wash it and cut into small pieces. Fill the measuring cup and reserve the rest for later. Set aside.

Wash the cucumber and cut into thin slices. Fill the measuring cup and reserve the rest for later.

Wash the zucchini and cut into small cubes. Set aside.

Now, combine bell pepper, lettuce,fennel, cucumber, and

zucchini in a juicer and process until juiced. Transfer to a serving glass and refrigerate for 5 minutes before serving.

Nutritional information per serving: Kcal: 85, Protein: 5.3g, Carbs: 25.2g, Fats: 1.1g

8. Cantaloupe Pear Juice

Ingredients:

1 cup of cantaloupe, peeled and chopped

1 medium-sized pear, chopped

1 whole leek, chopped

1 whole lime, peeled

1 oz of coconut water

¼ tsp of ginger, ground

Preparation:

Cut the cantaloupe in half. Scoop out the seeds and flesh. Cut and peel one large wedge. Chop into chunks and fill the measuring cup. Reserve the rest of the cantaloupe in a refrigerator.

Wash the pear lengthwise in half. Remove the core and cut into bite-sized pieces. Set aside.

Wash the leek thoroughly under cold running water. Drain and chop into small pieces. Set aside.

Peel the lime and cut lengthwise in half. Set aside.

Now, combine cantaloupe, pear, leek, and lime in a juicer

and process until juiced. Transfer to a serving glass and stir in the coconut water and ginger.

Add some ice, or refrigerate for 5 minutes before serving.

Nutritional information per serving: Kcal: 184, Protein: 3.5g, Carbs: 56.2g, Fats: 0.8g

9. Radish Brussels Sprout Juice

Ingredients:

2 large radishes, chopped

2 cups of Brussels sprouts, halved

1 small zucchini, chopped

1 cup of cucumber, sliced

2 large carrots, sliced

¼ tsp of turmeric, ground

Preparation:

Wash the radishes and trim off the green parts. Slightly peel and cut into small pieces. Set aside.

Wash the Brussels sprouts and trim off the outer layers. Cut into halves and fill the measuring cups. Reserve the rest in the refrigerator.

Wash the zucchini and cut into thin slices. Set aside.

Wash the cucumber and cut into thin slices. Fill the measuring cup and reserve the rest for later.

Wash and peel the carrots. Cut into thin slices and set aside.

Now, combine radishes, Brussels sprouts, zucchini, cucumber, and carrots in a juicer and process until juiced. Transfer to a serving glass and stir in the turmeric. Refrigerate for 15 minutes before serving.

Nutritional information per serving: Kcal: 118, Protein: 9.2g, Carbs: 35.7g, Fats: 1.3g

10. Swiss Chard Lime Juice

Ingredients:

½ cup of Swiss chard

1 large lime, peeled

½ cup of fresh basil

2 large green apples, cored

¼ cup of fresh mint

Preparation:

Wash the Swiss chard and basil thoroughly and roughly chop it. Set aside.

Peel the lime and cut into quarters. Set aside.

Wash the mint leaves and soak in water for 10 minutes. Set aside.

Wash the apples and remove the core. Cut into bite-sized pieces and set aside.

Now combine, Swiss chard, lime, basil, and apples, and mint in a juicer. Process until juiced. Transfer to serving glasses and add some ice before serving.

Garnish with some extra mint leaves and add some ice

before serving.

Enjoy!

Nutritional information per serving: Kcal: 114, Protein: 2.3g, Carbs: 30.4g, Fats: 0.2g

11. Pomegranate Apple Juice

Ingredients:

½ cup of pomegranate seeds

1 large green apple, cored

½ cup of fresh kale

¼ tsp of ginger, ground

3-4 fresh mint leaves

Preparation:

Cut the top of the pomegranate fruit using a sharp knife. slice down to each of the white membranes inside of the fruit. Pop the seeds into a medium sized bowl.

Wash the apple and remove the core. Cut into bite-sized pieces and set aside.

Wash thoroughly the kale. Drain and roughly chop it. Set aside.

Process the pomegranate seeds, apple, and kale in a juicer until well juiced.

Transfer to serving glasses and stir in the ginger. Add some water to adjust the thickness and garnish with mint leaves.

Add few ice cubes and serve immediately.

Nutritional information per serving: Kcal: 143, Protein: 6.2g, Carbs: 41.2g, Fats: 2.4g

12. Cucumber Pineapple Juice

Ingredients:

1 large cucumber

1 cup of pineapple, chopped

3 celery stalks

½ cup of fresh spinach

¼ tsp of ginger, ground

Preparation:

Wash and slice the cucumber into thick slices. Set aside.

Peel the pineapple and cut into chunks. Set aside.

Combine celery and spinach in a colander and wash under cold running water. Roughly chop the spinach and celery.

Combine cucumber, pineapple, celery, and spinach in a juicer and process until well juiced.

Transfer to serving glasses and stir in the ginger. Add a pinch of turmeric for some extra flavor. However, it's optional.

Serve immediately.

Nutritional information per serving: Kcal: 109, Protein: 3.3g, Carbs: 61.2g, Fats: 1.3g

13. Broccoli Carrot Juice

Ingredients:

1 cup of fresh broccoli

4 large carrots

2 cups of cauliflower, chopped

1 large green apple, cored

1 small ginger root slice, 1-inch

Preparation:

Wash the broccoli and chop it into small pieces.

Wash the carrots and cut into small pieces.

Wash the apple and remove the core. Cut into bite-sized pieces and set aside.

Wash the cauliflower under cold running water, and place it in a medium-sized bowl. Chop into small pieces and add water enough to cover it. Set aside to soak for 15 minutes.

Peel the ginger root and cut into halves.

Now, process cauliflower, broccoli, apple, carrot, and ginger root. Transfer to serving glasses and add some ice cubes before serving.

Enjoy!

Nutritional information per serving: Kcal: 136, Protein: 6.3g, Carbs: 42.8g, Fats: 1.2g

14. Sweet Potato Peach Juice

Ingredients:

2 medium-sized sweet potatoes, pre-cooked

1 large peach, pitted and halved

¼ tsp of ginger, ground

¼ tsp of cinnamon, ground

Preparation:

Peel the potatoes and place them in a pot of boiling water. Cook until fork-tender. Remove from the heat and drain well. Cut the potatoes into small pieces and set aside to cool completely.

Wash the peach and cut into halves. Remove the pit and chop into bite-sized pieces. Set aside.

Now, combine potatoes and peach in a juicer and process until juiced. Transfer to serving glasses and stir in the ginger and cinnamon.

Add some ice and serve immediately.

Nutritional information per serving: Kcal: 159, Protein: 5.2g, Carbs: 50.1g, Fats: 0.9g

15. Bok Choy Apple Juice

Ingredients:

1 small baby bok choy

1 large green apple, cored

¼ cup of fresh basil

1 medium-sized leek

2 large carrots

4-5 fresh kale leaves

Preparation:

Discard the ends of the bokchoy stems. Wash it thoroughly and chop it into small pieces. Set aside.

Wash the apple and remove the core. Cut into bite-sized pieces and set aside.

Wash the leek and chop into small pieces. set aside.

Combine basil and kale in a colander and wash under cold running water. Chop roughly with your hands. Set aside.

Wash the carrots and chop into thick slices. Set aside.

Now, process all prepared ingredients in a juicer. Transfer

to serving glasses and refrigerate for 10 minutes before serving.

Enjoy!

Nutritional information per serving: Kcal: 169, Protein: 2.3g, Carbs: 46.2g, Fats: 1.9g

16. Cantaloupe Lettuce Juice

Ingredients:

1 cup of cantaloupe, peeled

1 small Romaine lettuce head

1 tbsp of coconut, grated

½ cup of fresh basil

1 large cucumber

Preparation:

Peel the cantaloupe and cut into chunks. Reserve the rest of the cantaloupe in the refrigerator.

Wash the lettuce thoroughly. Roughly chop with hands and set aside.

Wash the cucumber and cut into thick slices. Set aside.

Wash the basil and chop with hands. Set aside.

Now, combine cantaloupe, lettuce, basil, and cucumber in a juicer and process until juiced.

Transfer to serving glasses and stir in the coconut. You can add some liquid honey for some extra taste, but this is optional.

Refrigerate for 15 minutes before serving.

Nutritional information per serving: Kcal: 112, Protein: 2.3g, Carbs: 22.6g, Fats: 1.1g

17. Mediterranean Citrus Juice

Ingredients:

½ tsp of fresh rosemary

3 large grapefruits, peeled

3 large oranges, peeled

1 whole lemon, peeled

Preparation:

Wash the grapefruits and cut into bite-sized pieces. Set aside.

Peel the oranges and divide into wedges. Set aside.

Peel the lemon and cut into quarters. Process in a juicer until well juiced.

Now, process grapefruits and oranges. Transfer to serving glasses and sprinkle with fresh rosemary for some extra flavor.

If you don't like rosemary, you can replace it with fresh mint.

Add some ice cubes and serve immediately.

Enjoy!

Nutritional information per serving: Kcal: 140, Protein: 3.4g, Carbs: 37.6g, Fats: 0.1g

18. Orange Cucumber Juice

Ingredients:

2 large oranges, peeled

1 large cucumber, peeled

1 cup of broccoli

1 large carrot, sliced

Preparation:

Peel the oranges and cut into wedges.

Peel the cucumber and cut into bite-sized pieces and aside.

Wash the broccoli thoroughly. Cut into bite-sized pieces and set aside.

Wash and cut the carrot into thin slices. Process in a juicer until juiced. Now, continue to process broccoli, orange wedges, and cucumber.

Stir well with a spoon and add some ice cubes before serving.

Nutritional information per serving: Kcal: 68, Protein: 2.3g, Carbs: 19.7g, Fats: 0.1g

19. Fennel Pepper Juice

Ingredients:

1 large fennel bulb, trimmed

2 cups of fresh asparagus, trimmed

1 large green bell pepper, seeded

1 large yellow bell pepper, seeded

1 ginger root slice, 1-inch

2 oz of water

Preparation:

Wash the fennel bulb and trim off the wilted outer layers. Cut into small chunks and set aside.

Wash the bell peppers and cut in half. Remove the seeds and cut into small slices. Set aside.

Wash the asparagus and trim off the woody ends. Cut into 1-inch pieces and set aside.

Peel the ginger root slice and set aside.

Now, combine asparagus, fennel, green and yellow bell pepper, and ginger root in a juicer and process until juiced.

Transfer to serving glasses and stir in the water. Refrigerate for 5 minutes before serving and enjoy!

Nutrition information per serving: Kcal: 143, Protein: 12.1g, Carbs: 47.2g, Fats: 1.5g

20. Zucchini Lemon Juice

Ingredients:

1 large zucchini, chopped

1 large lemon, peeled

1 cup of pumpkin

1 medium-sized yellow apple, cored

1 medium-sized banana

2 oz of water

Preparation:

Peel the zucchini and cut in half. Scrape out the seeds with a spoon. Cut into chunks and set aside.

Peel the lemon and cut lengthwise in half. Set aside.

Peel the pumpkin and cut in half. Scoop out the seeds using a spoon. Cut one large wedge and peel it. Cut into small chunks and set aside. Reserve the rest for later.

Wash the apple and remove the core. Cut into bite-sized pieces and set aside.

Peel the banana and cut into small chunks. Set aside.

Now, process zucchini, lemon, pumpkin, apple, and banana in a juicer. Transfer to serving glasses and stir in the water.

Add some ice and serve immediately.

Nutrition information per serving: Kcal: 254, Protein: 7.5g, Carbs: 72.9g, Fats: 1.9g

21. Green Celery Juice

Ingredients:

1 cup of celery

1 cup of Swiss chards

1 medium-sized apple, cored

1 cup of collard greens

2 tbsp of fresh parsley

4-5 fresh spinach leaves

2 oz of water

Preparation:

Combine Swiss chards, collard greens, celery, and spinach in a colander. Wash thoroughly under cold running water and drain. Torn with hands and set aside.

Wash the apple and remove the core. Cut into bite-sized pieces and set aside.

Now, combine Swiss chards, celery, apple, collard greens, and spinach in a juicer and process until juiced.

Transfer to serving glasses and stir in the water. Add some ice and garnish with fresh parsley.

Enjoy!

Nutrition information per serving: Kcal: 106, Protein: 4.8g, Carbs: 31.3g, Fats: 1.1g

22. Broccoli Artichoke Juice

Ingredients:

1 cup of fresh broccoli

1 large artichoke head

1 cup of Brussels sprouts, trimmed

1 large lemon, peeled

1 large cucumber

3 tbsp of fresh parsley

Preparation:

Wash the broccoli and chop into small pieces. set aside.

Using a sharp knife, trim off the outer layers of the artichoke. Wash it and cut into bite-sized pieces. Set aside.

Wash the Brussels sprouts and trim off the outer layers. Cut in half and set aside.

Peel the lemon and cut lengthwise in half. Set aside.

Wash the cucumber and cut into thick slices. Set aside.

Now, process Brussels sprouts, broccoli, artichoke, lemon, and cucumber in a juicer.

Transfer to serving glasses and garnish with fresh parsley. Refrigerate for 10 minutes before serving.

Enjoy!

Nutrition information per serving: Kcal: 140, Protein: 13.8g, Carbs: 48.1g, Fats: 1.4g

23. Apple Lemon Juice

Ingredients:

2 medium-sized Golden Delicious apples

1 large lemon, peeled

1 large cucumber

3 medium-sized celery stalks

A handful of spinach

2 oz of water

Preparation:

Wash the apples and remove the core. Cut into bite-sized pieces and set aside.

Peel the lemon and cut lengthwise in half. Set aside.

Wash the cucumber and cut into thick slices. Set aside.

Wash the celery stalks and cut into 1-inch pieces. Set aside.

Wash the spinach thoroughly and torn with hands. Set aside.

Now, process apples, lemon, cucumber, celery, and spinach in a juicer. Transfer to serving glasses and stir in the water.

Add some ice and serve.

Nutrition information per serving: Kcal: 224, Protein: 5.2g, Carbs: 65.4g, Fats: 1.5g

24. Swiss Chard Cucumber Juice

Ingredients:

2 cups of Swiss chard

1 large cucumber

1 cup of fresh parsley, torn

1 small yellow apple, cored

1 small orange, peeled

Preparation:

Combine parsley and Swiss chard in a colander and wash thoroughly under cold running water. Drain and torn with hands. Set aside.

Wash the cucumber and cut into thick slices. Set aside.

Wash the apple and remove the core. Cut into bite-sized pieces and set aside.

Peel the orange and divide into wedges. Set aside.

Now, combine parsley, Swiss chard, cucumber apple, and orange in a juicer and process until juiced. Transfer to serving glasses and add some ice before serving.

Enjoy!

Nutrition information per serving: Kcal: 161, Protein: 6.3g, Carbs: 46.3g, Fats: 1.2g

25. Mint Arugula Juice

Ingredients:

1 cup of fresh mint

1 cup of fresh arugula

1 large carrot

1 large orange, peeled

1 large red bell pepper, seeded

Preparation:

Combine mint and arugula in a colander and wash thoroughly under cold running water. Drain and torn with hands. Set aside.

Wash the carrot and cut into thick slices. Set aside.

Peel the orange and divide into wedges. Set aside.

Wash the bell pepper and cut in half. Remove the seeds and chop into small slices. Set aside.

Now, combine mint, arugula, carrot, orange, and bell pepper in a juicer and process until juiced.

Transfer to serving glasses and stir in the water. You can add a pinch of Himalayan salt, but this is optional.

Add some ice and serve immediately.

Nutrition information per serving: Kcal: 153, Protein: 7.9g, Carbs: 47.3g, Fats: 1.3g

26. Plum Ginger Juice

Ingredients:

5 large plums, pitted

1 cup of fresh broccoli

1 large cucumber

1 medium-sized apple, cored

¼ tsp of ginger, ground

Preparation:

Wash the plums and cut in half. Remove the pits and set aside.

Wash the broccoli and cut into small pieces. Set aside.

Wash the cucumber and cut into thick slices and set aside.

Wash the apple and remove the core. Cut into bite-sized pieces and set aside.

Now, combine plums, broccoli, cucumber, and apple in a juicer and process until juiced.

Transfer to serving glasses and stir in the ginger. Add few ice cubes before serving.

Enjoy!

Nutrition information per serving: Kcal: 268, Protein: 7.6g, Carbs: 77.4g, Fats: 1.9g

27. Pomegranate Lime Juice

Ingredients:

1 cup of pomegranate seeds

1 large lime, peeled

1 cup of beets, trimmed and chopped

2 large carrots

1 large cucumber

Preparation:

Cut the top of the pomegranate fruit using a sharp knife. Slice down to each of the white membranes inside of the fruit. Pop the seeds into a measuring cup and set aside.

Peel the lime and cut into lengthwise in half. Set aside.

Wash the beets and trim off the green parts. Cut into bite-sized pieces and fill the measuring cup. Reserve the rest for some other juice.

Wash the carrot and cucumber and cut into thick slices. Set aside.

Now, process pomegranate seeds, lime, beets, carrots and cucumber in a juicer.

Transfer to serving glasses and stir in the water. Add some ice and serve!

Nutrition information per serving: Kcal: 194, Protein: 7.2g, Carbs: 57.7g, Fats: 1.9g

28. Beet Cauliflower Juice

Ingredients:

3 large beets, trimmed

1 cup of cauliflower, chopped

2 cups of green grapes

1 large lemon, peeled

Preparation:

Wash the beets and trim off the green parts. Cut into bite-sized pieces and set

aside.

Trim off the outer leaves of cauliflower. Wash it and cut into small pieces. Fill the measuring cup and reserve the rest for some other juice. Set aside.

Wash the green grapes under cold running water. Set aside.

Peel the lemon and cut lengthwise in half. Set aside.

Now, process beets, grapes, cauliflower, and lemon in a juicer.

Transfer to serving glasses and add some ice cubes before

serving.

Enjoy!

Nutrition information per serving: Kcal: 226, Protein: 7.8g, Carbs: 65.8g, Fats: 1.5g

29. Orange Carrot Juice

Ingredients:

4 large oranges, peeled

1 cup of carrots, sliced

1 cup of broccoli, chopped

1 cup of Brussels sprouts, chopped

1 cup of turnip greens, chopped

1 tbsp of honey

¼ cup of pure coconut water

Preparation:

Peel the oranges and divide into wedges. Set aside.

Wash the carrots and cut into thick slices. Set aside.

Wash the broccoli and cut into small pieces. Set aside.

Wash the Brussels sprouts and trim off the outer layers. Cut in half and set aside.

Wash the turnip greens thoroughly and torn with hands. Set aside.

Now, combine broccoli, Brussels sprouts, carrots, turnip

greens, and oranges in a juicer and process until juiced.

Transfer to serving glasses and stir in the honey and coconut water. Add some ice cubes before serving or refrigerate for 5 minutes.

Enjoy!

Nutrition information per serving: Kcal: 367, Protein: 14.47g, Carbs: 116g, Fats: 1.9g

30. Blackberry Orange Juice

Ingredients:

1 cup of blackberries, fresh

1 large orange, peeled

2 wedges of watermelon, seeded

½ cup of pure coconut water, unsweetened

1 tbsp of honey, raw

Preparation:

Wash the blackberries under cold running water and set aside.

Peel the orange and divide into wedges. Set aside.

Cut the watermelon lengthwise. Cut two large wedges and peel them. Cut into chunks and remove the seeds. Set aside.

Now, combine watermelon, blackberries, and orange in a juicer and process until juiced.

Transfer to serving glasses and stir the coconut water and honey.

Refrigerate for 5 minutes before serving.

Enjoy!

Nutrition information per serving: Kcal: 264, Protein: 7.2g, Carbs: 78.6g, Fats: 1.7g

31. Tomato Pepper Juice

Ingredients:

2 large tomatoes, peeled

1 cup of red bell peppers, chopped and seeds removed

4 cups of watercress, torn

4 cups of red leaf lettuce, torn

¼ cup of water

Preparation:

Wash the tomatoes and place them in a bowl. Cut into quarters and reserve the juice while cutting. Set aside.

Wash the bell peppers and cut in half. Remove the seeds and roughly chop it. Fill the measuring cup and reserve the rest for some other juice. Set aside.

Combine watercress and red leaf lettuce in a colander. Wash thoroughly under cold running water and torn with hands. Set aside.

Now, combine tomatoes, bell pepper, watercress, and red leaf lettuce in a juicer and process until juiced.

Transfer to serving glasses and stir in the reserved tomato

juice and water.

Refrigerate for 5 minutes before serving.

Enjoy!

Nutrition information per serving: Kcal: 106, Protein: 9.2g, Carbs: 27.4g, Fats: 1.5g

32. Lemon Zucchini Juice

Ingredients:

1 whole lemon, peeled and halved

1 small zucchini, thinly sliced

1 cup of cauliflower, chopped

1 medium artichoke, chopped

1 small ginger knob, chopped

¼ tsp salt

Preparation:

Peel the lemon and cut lengthwise in half. Set aside.

Wash the zucchini and thinly slice it. Set aside.

Trim off the outer layer of the cauliflower. Cut into bite-sized pieces and wash it. Fill the measuring cup and sprinkle with some salt. Set aside.

Trim off the outer layers of the artichoke using a sharp paring knife. Cut into bite-sized pieces and set aside.

Peel the ginger knob and chop into small pieces. Set aside.

Now, combine lemon, zucchini, cauliflower, artichoke, and

ginger in a juicer. Process until well juiced.

Transfer to a serving glass and refrigerate for 10 minutes before serving.

Enjoy!

Nutrition information per serving: Kcal: 82, Protein: 8.4g, Carbs: 28.9g, Fats: 1.1g

33. Broccoli Parsley Juice

Ingredients:

2 cups of broccoli, chopped

1 cup of fresh parsley, torn

1 cup of beets, trimmed and chopped

1 cup of celery, chopped

¼ tsp of turmeric, ground

¼ tsp ginger, ground

Preparation:

Wash the broccoli and trim off the outer layers. Chop into small pieces and set aside.

Rinse the parsley under cold running water and slightly drain. Torn with hands into small pieces and set aside.

Wash and peel the beets. Trim off the green ends and chop into bite-sized pieces. Fill the measuring cup and reserve the rest for later.

Wash the celery stalks and chop it into bite-sized pieces. Fill the measuring cup and set aside.

Now, combine broccoli, parsley, beets, and celery in a

juicer and process until juiced. Transfer to a serving glass and stir in the turmeric and ginger.

Refrigerate for 5 minutes before serving.

Nutrition information per serving: Kcal: 109, Protein: 9.8g, Carbs: 31.8g, Fats: 1.5g

34. Banana Blackberry Juice

Ingredients:

1 cup of blackberries

1 large banana, chunked

1 cup of mango, chunked

1 large orange, peeled

¼ tsp of cinnamon, ground

Preparation:

Place the blackberries in a colander and wash under cold running water. Slightly drain and set aside.

Peel the banana and cut into small chunks. Set aside.

Wash the mango and cut into small chunks. Fill the measuring cup and reserve the rest for later.

Peel the orange and divide into wedges. Cut each wedge in half and set aside.

Now, combine mango, blackberries, banana, and orange in a juicer and process until juiced. Transfer to a serving glass and stir in the cinnamon.

Add few ice cubes and serve immediately.

Nutrition information per serving: Kcal: 296, Protein: 6.6g, Carbs: 91.2g, Fats: 2.1g

35. Lime Blueberry Juice

Ingredients:

1 whole lime, peeled

1 cup of blueberries

1 cup of fresh spinach, chopped

1 medium-sized orange

1 oz coconut water

1 tbsp fresh mint, torn

Preparation:

Peel the lime and cut lengthwise in half. Set aside.

Place the blueberries in a colander and wash under cold running water. Slightly drain and set aside.

Wash the spinach thoroughly and drain. Chop into small pieces and set aside.

Peel the orange and divide into wedges. Cut each wedge in half and set aside.

Now, combine blueberries, spinach, lime, and orange in a juicer and process until well juiced. Transfer to a serving glass and stir in the coconut water.

Sprinkle with some fresh mint and serve.

Enjoy!

Nutrition information per serving: Kcal: 158, Protein: 8.5g, Carbs: 48.1g, Fats: 1.5g

36. Tomato Basil Juice

Ingredients:

1 cup of cherry tomatoes, halved

1 cup of Swiss chard, torn

1 cup of basil, torn

1 cup of beets, trimmed

¼ tsp of balsamic vinegar

¼ tsp of salt

1 oz of water

Preparation:

Wash the cherry tomatoes and remove the green stems. Cut in half and fill the measuring cup. Reserve the rest in the refrigerator for some other juice.

Combine basil and Swiss chard in a large colander and rinse thoroughly under cold running water. Drain and torn with hands into small pieces. Set aside.

Wash the beets and trim off the green parts. Cut into thin slices and fill the measuring cup. Reserve the rest for later.

Now, combine cherry tomatoes, Swiss chard, basil, and

beets in a juicer and process until juiced. Transfer to a serving glass and stir in the vinegar, salt, and water.

Serve immediately.

Nutrition information per serving: Kcal: 72, Protein: 5.1g, Carbs: 21.6g, Fats: 0.7g

37. Orange Pear Juice

Ingredients:

1 medium-sized orange, peeled

1 medium-sized pear, chopped

1 cup of fennel, chopped

1 whole lemon, peeled

¼ tsp of cinnamon, ground

1 oz of coconut water

Preparation:

Peel the orange and divide into wedges. Cut each wedge in half and set aside.

Wash the pear and cut in half. Remove the core and cut into small pieces. Set aside.

Trim off the outer wilted layers of the fennel. Roughly chop it and fill the measuring cup. Reserve the rest for later.

Peel the lemon and cut lengthwise in half. Set aside.

Now, combine orange, pear, fennel, and lemon in a juicer and process until well juiced. Transfer to a serving glass and stir in the cinnamon and coconut water.

Refrigerate for 10 minutes before serving.

Enjoy!

Nutrition information per serving: Kcal: 156, Protein: 3.6g, Carbs: 54.2g, Fats: 0.7g

38. Carrot Lemon Juice

Ingredients:

1 large carrot, sliced

1 whole lemon, peeled

1 cup of celery, chopped

1 small Granny Smith's apple, cored

¼ tsp ginger, ground

Preparation:

Wash and peel the carrot. Cut into small slices and set aside.

Wash the celery and cut into small pieces. Set aside.

Peel the lemon and cut lengthwise in half. Set aside.

Wash the apple and cut in half. Remove the core and cut into bite-sized pieces. Set aside.

Now, combine carrot, celery, lemon, and apple in a juicer and process until juiced. Transfer to a serving glass and stir in the water and ginger. Refrigerate for 5 minutes.

Serve immediately.

Nutrition information per serving: Kcal: 105, Protein: 2.4g, Carbs: 32.8g, Fats: 0.7g

39. Pear Cucumber Juice

Ingredients:

1 large pear, chopped

1 whole cucumber, sliced

1 cup of purple cabbage, chopped

1 whole lemon, peeled

Preparation:

Wash the pear and cut lengthwise in half. Remove the core and chop into small pieces. Set aside.

Wash the cucumber and cut into thin slices. Set aside.

Wash the cabbage thoroughly under cold running water. Drain and chop into small pieces. Set aside.

Peel the lemon and cut lengthwise in half. Set aside.

Now, combine pear, cucumber, cabbage, and lemon in a juicer. Process until well juiced. Transfer to a serving glass and serve immediately.

Enjoy!

Nutrition information per serving: Kcal: 173, Protein: 4.7g, Carbs: 57.9g, Fats: 0.9g

40. Kale Pomegranate Juice

Ingredients:

1 cup of fresh kale, torn

1 cup of pomegranate seeds

2 cups of Swiss chard, torn

1 large orange, peeled

1 small Golden Delicious apple, cored

Preparation:

Cut the top of the pomegranate fruit using a sharp paring knife. Slice down to each of the white membranes inside of the fruit. Pop the seeds into a measuring cup and set aside.

Combine Swiss chard and kale in a large colander. Rinse under cold running water and drain. Torn into small pieces and set aside.

Peel the orange and divide into wedges. Cut each wedge in half and set aside.

Wash the apple and cut lengthwise in half. Remove the core and cut into bite-sized pieces. Set aside.

Now, combine Swiss chard, kale, pomegranate seeds,

orange, and apple in a juicer and process until juiced. Transfer to a serving glass and add few ice cubes.

Serve immediately.

Nutrition information per serving: Kcal: 227, Protein: 7.9g, Carbs: 66.1g, Fats: 2.3g

41. Salted Avocado Zucchini Juice

Ingredients:

1 cup of avocado, cubed

1 small zucchini, sliced

3 large radishes, chopped

1 cup of celery, chopped

1 cup of cucumber, sliced

¼ tsp of salt

1 oz of water

Preparation:

Peel the avocado and cut in half. Remove the pit and cut into small cubes. Fill the measuring cup and reserve the rest for later.

Wash the zucchini and cut into thin slices. Set aside.

Wash the radishes and cut into small pieces. Set aside.

Wash the celery and chop it into bite-sized pieces. Set aside.

Wash the cucumber and cut into thin slices. Fill the

measuring cup and reserve the rest for later. Set aside.

Now, combine avocado, radishes, zucchini, celery, and cucumber in a juicer and process until juiced. Transfer to a serving glass and stir in the salt and water.

Serve immediately.

Nutrition information per serving: Kcal: 235, Protein: 5.6g, Carbs: 22.3g, Fats: 22.6g

42. Artichoke Lime Juice

Ingredients:

1 medium-sized artichoke, chopped

1 whole lime, peeled

1 cup of basil, torn

1 cup of cucumber, sliced

2 oz of water

Preparation:

Trim off the outer leaves of the artichoke. Wash it and chop into small pieces. Set aside.

Peel the lime and cut lengthwise in half. Set aside.

Wash the basil thoroughly under cold running water. Drain and torn into small pieces. Set aside.

Wash the cucumber and cut into thin slices. Fill the measuring cup and reserve the rest in the refrigerator.

Now, combine artichoke, lime, basil, and cucumber in a juicer and process until juiced. Transfer to a serving glass and stir in the water.

Refrigerate for 5 minutes before serving.

Nutrition information per serving: Kcal: 53, Protein: 5.5g, Carbs: 19.6g, Fats: 0.4g

43. Tomato Collard Green Juice

Ingredients:

1 large tomato

1 cup of collard greens, torn

2 cups of parsnips, trimmed

1 large yellow bell pepper, seeded

1 large cucumber

Preparation:

Wash the tomato and place in a bowl. Cut into quarters and reserve the juice while cutting. Set aside.

Wash the collard greens thoroughly and torn with hands. Set aside.

Wash the parsnips and cut into thick slices. Set aside.

Wash the bell pepper and cut in half. Remove the seeds and cut into small pieces. Set aside.

Wash the cucumber and cut into thick slices. Set aside.

Now, process parsnips, bell pepper, tomato, collard greens, and cucumber in a juicer.

Transfer to serving glasses and stir in the reserved tomato juice.

Refrigerate for 10 minutes before serving.

Nutritional information per serving: Kcal: 254, Protein: 9.5g, Carbs: 77.7g, Fats: 2.2g

44. Spinach Cilantro Juice

Ingredients:

½ cup of fresh spinach

½ cup of fresh cilantro

½ cup of fresh arugula

3-4 celery stalks

1 large green apple, cored

Preparation:

Combine spinach, cilantro, and arugula in a large colander. Wash under cold running water and drain. Torn into small pieces and set aside.

Wash the celery stalks and cut into small pieces. Set aside.

Wash the apple and remove the core. Cut into bite-sized pieces and set aside.

Now, combine arugula, cilantro, spinach, celery, and apple in a juicer and process until juiced.

Transfer to serving glasses and add few ice cubes before serving.

Enjoy!

Nutritional information per serving: Kcal: 61, Protein: 2.1g, Carbs: 20.2g, Fats: 1.2g

45. Cherry Lemon Juice

Ingredients:

1 cup of fresh cherries, pitted

1 large lemon, peeled

1 cup of mango, cubed

1 cup of watermelon, cubed

1 tbsp of liquid honey

2 oz of water

Preparation:

Wash the cherries under cold running water. Drain and cut in half. Remove the pits and set aside.

Peel the lemon and cut lengthwise in half. Set aside.

Peel the mango and cut into small chunks. Set aside.

Cut the watermelon lengthwise. For one cup, you will need about 1 large wedge. Peel and cut into chunks. Remove the seeds and set aside. Reserve the rest of the melon for some other juices.

Now, process cherries, mango, lemon, and watermelon in a juicer.

Transfer to serving glasses and add few ice cubes before serving.

Enjoy!

Nutrition information per serving: Kcal: 288, Protein: 4.6g, Carbs: 68.3g, Fats: 1.3g

46. Orange Squash Juice

Ingredients:

1 large orange, peeled

1 cup of butternut squash, cubed

1 cup of avocado, peeled, pitted, and cubed

1 cup of fresh basil

1 large lime, peeled

2 oz of coconut water

Preparation:

Peel the orange and divide into wedges. Set aside.

Peel the butternut squash and remove the seeds using a spoon. Cut into small cubes and reserve the rest of the squash for some other recipe. Wrap in a plastic foil and refrigerate.

Peel the avocado in half. Remove the pit and cut into small chunks. Set aside.

Wash the basil thoroughly and torn with hands. Set aside.

Peel the lime and cut lengthwise in half. Set aside.

Now, process avocado, squash, basil, orange, and lime in a juicer.

Transfer to serving glasses and add few ice cubes before serving.

Nutrition information per serving: Kcal: 339, Protein: 6.9g, Carbs: 56.7g, Fats: 21.9g

SALAD RECIPES

1. Avocado Eggs with Greens

Ingredients:

1 avocado, halved and pitted

2 eggs

2 tbsp freshly squeezed lime juice

1 tsp dried thyme

½ tsp dried rosemary

¼ tsp red pepper flakes

¼ tsp sea salt

1 large tomato, chopped into chunks

1 cup lettuce, torn

1 cup baby spinach, chopped

1 cup arugula, chopped

Preparation:

Rinse lettuce, spinach, and arugula under cold running

water and set aside to drain in a large colander.

Preheat the oven to 400 degrees. Line a small square baking pan with some parchment paper and set aside.

Cut avocado in half and remove the pit. Place avocado halves in a baking pan and brush with the lime juice. Slowly pour the eggs into each hole and sprinkle with thyme, rosemary, salt, and red pepper flakes.

Bake for 15 minutes or until set. Remove from the oven and cool for a while.

Meanwhile, in a large bowl, toss together tomato, lettuce, spinach, and arugula. Sprinkle with the remaining lime juice and serve with avocado.

Nutritional information per serving: Kcal: 205, Protein: 6.2g, Carbs: 12.4g, Fats: 16.3g

2. Egg Salad with Spinach and Nuts

Ingredients:

1 lb fresh spinach, torn

2 garlic cloves, crushed

½ tsp sea salt

2 eggs, hard-boiled

5 almonds, finely chopped

5 walnuts, finely chopped

¼ tsp chili flakes

Olive oil for the pan

Preparation:

Gently place eggs in a pot of boiling water. Cook for 10-12 minutes. Remove from the heat and drain. Cool to a room temperature and peel. Using a sharp knife, cut eggs in half. Set aside.

Now grease a large non-stick skillet with some olive oil and heat up over medium-high heat. Add garlic and stir-fry for two minutes. Add spinach and continue to cook for five minutes, stirring constantly. Season with chili flakes, give it a good stir and remove from the heat. Transfer to a serving plate and sprinkle with sea salt, chopped almonds, and walnuts.

Serve with boiled eggs. Optionally, add ½ cup of avocado chunks!

Nutritional information per serving: Kcal: 185, Protein: 14.7g, Carbs: 11g, Fats: 11.4g

3. Turkey Breast Salad

Ingredients:

8 oz boneless and skinless turkey breast, sliced into 1-inch thick slices

2 cups arugula

2 tbsp goat's cheese

5 almonds

5 walnuts

2 tbsp red wine vinegar

1 tbsp dried thyme

1 tomato, sliced

Preparation:

Remove the breast from the refrigerator about 30 minutes before use. Cover and let them it at the room temperature.

Preheat a non-stick grill pan to medium-high. Brush with some olive oil and add sliced turkey. Cook for 7-8 minutes or until lightly charred, turning halfway through.

Remove from the heat and cool for about five minutes while you assemble the salad.

In a small bowl, whisk together red wine vinegar, dried thyme, and olive oil. Set aside.

In a large bowl, combine together arugula, tomato, goat's cheese, almonds, and walnuts. Top with turkey breast and drizzle with the red wine mixture.

Serve immediately.

Nutritional information per serving: Kcal: 277, Protein: 28g, Carbs: 9.4g, Fats: 14.2g

4. Garlic Chicken and Vegetable Salad

Ingredients:

1lb chicken breast, sliced into half-inch thick slices

½ cup freshly squeezed lime juice

2 tbsp olive oil

½ cup parsley leaves, finely chopped

3 garlic cloves, crushed

1 tbsp cayenne pepper

1 tsp dried oregano

½ tsp sea salt

1 cup cherry tomatoes, sliced

1 cup arugula, chopped

1 cup lamb's lettuce, chopped

Preparation:

Rinse the meat under cold running water and drain in a large colander. Using a sharp knife, slice into approximately half-inch thick slices. Set aside.

In a medium bowl, combine olive oil with lime juice,

chopped parsley, crushed garlic, cayenne pepper, oregano, and salt.

Generously brush fillets with this mixture and cover. Refrigerate for 30 minutes.

Preheat a large, non-stick frying pan over medium-high heat. Remove the fillets from the marinade and pat-dry with a kitchen towel. Cook for 4-5 minutes on each side.

In a large bowl, combine together tomatoes, arugula, and lamb's lettuce. Add chicken and optionally, sprinkle with some lemon or lime juice.

Serve immediately.

Nutritional information per serving: Kcal: 283, Protein: 33.6g, Carbs: 6.2g, Fats: 13.7g

5. Chicken and Button Mushrooms Salad

Ingredients:

1lb chicken breast, cut into bite-sized pieces

3.5 oz button mushrooms, whole

1 medium-sized tomato, roughly chopped

2 oz lettuce

1 cucumber, sliced

1 tbsp olive oil

1 tbsp Dijon mustard

2 tbsp apple cider vinegar

1 tsp freshly squeezed lemon juice

1 tbsp dried rosemary

½ tsp pink Himalayan salt

Kalamata olives (optional for serving)

Cooking spray

Preparation:

Rinse the meat under cold running water and pat dry with

a kitchen towel. Place on a cutting board and chop into bite-sized pieces. Set aside.

In a small bowl, combine Dijon mustard with olive oil, dried rosemary, apple cider, and salt. Stir well and brush the meat with this mixture. Wrap in aluminum foil and refrigerate for 30 minutes.

Meanwhile, spray a large, non-stick skillet with some cooking spray. Add button mushrooms and cook for 10 minutes, stirring occasionally. Remove from the heat and cool to a room temperature. Wash and prepare the vegetables. Place in a serving bowl. Add mushrooms and stir well. Set aside. Preheat the oven to 350 degrees. Line some parchment paper over a baking pan and set aside.

Remove the meat from the refrigerator and transfer into a baking pan along with the marinade. Cook for 35 minutes, turning once. When done, remove the meat from the oven and chill to a room temperature. Serve with vegetables.

Nutritional information per serving: Kcal: 254, Protein: 34.5g, Carbs: 8g, Fats: 9.2g

6. Tuna Salad

Ingredients:

1 cup tuna, canned in water

3 eggs, hard-boiled

1 cucumber, sliced

¼ cup walnuts

½ cup fresh goat's cheese

1 cup baby spinach, finely chopped

½ carrot, sliced

1 tbsp freshly squeezed lemon juice

½ tsp salt

Preparation:

Gently place eggs in the pot of boiling water. Cook for 12 minutes. Remove from the heat and drain. Chill to a room temperature and peel. Slice one egg in half and chop the remaining two. Place in a serving plate.

Add vegetables and season with salt. Drizzle with lemon juice and top with tuna and the remaining egg.

Serve immediately.

Nutritional information per serving: Kcal: 208, Protein: 19.4g, Carbs: 4.9g, Fats: 12.7g

7. Warm Quinoa with Nuts and Cranberries

Ingredients:

1 cup quinoa

3 tbsp hazelnuts, minced

½ cup fresh parsley

1 small onion, finely chopped

2 garlic cloves, crushed

¼ tsp salt

2 tbsp olive oil

1 cup button mushrooms, sliced

¼ cup cranberries

Preparation:

Grease a small skillet with some olive oil or cooking spray and heat up over medium-high heat. Add sliced mushrooms and cook for 6-7 minutes, stirring constantly. Remove from the heat and season with salt. Set aside.

Add quinoa to a small, heavy-bottomed pan and pour in one cup of water. Bring to a boil over medium heat and gently simmer until all the liquid has evaporated. Stir occasionally.

When done, remove from the heat and cool for a while.

In a small bowl, combine together hazelnuts, parsley, salt, and one tablespoon of olive oil. Mix all well and add chopped onions and crushed garlic. Let it sit for 5-10 minutes.

Stir in cooked quinoa and mushrooms. Top with cranberries and mix well to combine. Serve immediately.

Nutritional information per serving: Kcal: 206, Protein: 6.1g, Carbs: 25.3g, Fats: 9.5g

8. Cucumber and Parsley Salad with Lime

Ingredients:

1 large cucumber, thinly sliced

2 garlic cloves, crushed

¼ cup fresh parsley, chopped

1 tbsp fresh lime juice

2 tbsp extra virgin olive oil

Salt and pepper to taste

Preparation:

In a small bowl, combine together garlic, lime juice, olive oil, and some salt and pepper. Mix all well and let it sit for 10 minutes.

Meanwhile, peel and thinly slice cucumber. Transfer to a bowl and sprinkle with freshly chopped parsley.

Drizzle with the garlic oil and optionally season with some more salt or pepper to taste.

Refrigerate for at least 30 minutes before serving.

Nutritional information per serving: Kcal: 299, Protein: 2.8g, Carbs: 13.9g, Fats: 28.5g

9. Brown Rice Salad

Ingredients:

1 cup brown rice

3 spring onions, finely chopped

½ cup corn

1 red bell pepper, cut into strips

¼ cup fresh mint, finely chopped

2 tbsp extra virgin olive oil

1 tbsp apple cider vinegar

Salt to taste

Preparation:

Add rice in a medium saucepan and pour in two cups of cold water. Cover with the lid and bring to a boil over medium heat. Reduce the heat to low and cover with the lid. Cook over low heat for 15-18 minutes, stirring occasoanlly.

When done, turn off the heat and let the rice sit covered for another 10-15 minutes.

Meanwhile, drain corn in a small sieve and transfer to a

serving bowl. Prepare the vegetables. Cut pepper in half and remove stem and seeds. Cut into strips and add to a bowl. Finely chop onions and toss with corn and pepper.

Finally, add rice and stir in mint. Sprinkle with olive oil, apple cider vinegar, and some salt to taste.

Mix all well and serve.

Nutritional information per serving: Kcal: 353, Protein: 6.5g, Carbs: 57.9g, Fats: 11.5g

10. Fresh Vegetable Salad

Ingredients:

2 cups lettuce, torn

1 purple onion, diced

1 medium tomato, chopped

1 green bell pepper, diced

1 small chili, diced

1 cup baby spinach, chopped

2 tbsp extra virgin olive oil

1 tbsp apple cider vinegar

1 tsp fresh rosemary, finely chopped

¼ tsp salt

Preparation:

Add lettuce and baby spinach to a large colander and rinse thoroughly under cold running water. Set aside to drain.

Now, prepare the vegetables. Rinse tomato and pat dry with a kitchen towel. Chop into bite-sized pieces and add to serving bowl.

Cut green pepper in half and remove the seeds. Using a sharp knife, dice the pepepr and transfer to a bowl.

Dice onion and one small chili. Add all to a bowl and top with drained greens. Sprinkle with olive oil, apple cider vinegar, rosemary, and salt.

Mix all well and serve immediately.

Nutritional information per serving: Kcal: 196, Protein: 2.9g, Carbs: 15.6g, Fats: 15g

11. Sweet Carrot Salad

Ingredients:

1 medium-sized carrot, sliced

2oz baby spinach

1 medium-sized tomato, finely chopped

2oz rice spaghetti, soaked

1 small cucumber, finely chopped

¼ cup fresh blueberries

¼ cup honey

¼ cup fresh lime juice

1 tsp Dijon mustard

¼ tbsp ground cumin

Preparation:

Place the rice spaghetti in a deep pot and pour water enough to cover. Soak the rice spaghetti in water for about 15 minutes. Drain and transfer to a bowl. Set aside.

Rinse the spinach under running water and drain. Chop into small pieces and set aside.

Wash the tomato and chop into small pieces. Set aside.

In a large salad bowl, add chopped spinach, tomato, sliced carrot, and blueberries. Toss to combine.

In a small mixing bowl, combine honey, lime juice, Dijon mustard, and cumin. Mix until combined and drizzle over salad. Toss to combine and serve immediately.

Enjoy!

Nutritional information per serving: Kcal: 201, Protein: 3.4g, Carbs: 48.6g, Fats: 0.7g

12. Spring Salad with Black Olives

Ingredients:

5 cherry tomatoes

A handful of black olives

1 medium-sized onion, peeled and sliced

2 radishes, sliced

A handful of lamb's lettuce

2 tbsp freshly squeezed lime juice

3 tbsp extra virgin olive oil

Salt to taste

Preparation:

In a small mixing bowl, combine olive oil, lime juice, and salt. Mix until well combined and set aside.

Rinse the tomatoes and remove the stems. Cut into halves and set aside.

Wash the radishes and trim off the green parts. Cut into thin slices and set aside.

Rinse the lettuce using a large colander. Drain and chop

into small pieces.

In a large salad bowl, combine tomatoes, olives, onion, radishes, and lamb's lettuce. Drizzle with previously prepared dressing.

Toss to combine and serve immediately.

Nutritional information per serving: Kcal: 197, Protein: 2.7g, Carbs: 15.3g, Fats: 15.7g

13. Crispy Beans Salad with Lime Dressing

Ingredients:

½ red onion, peeled and sliced

2 oz green beans, cooked

3 cherry tomatoes, halved

1 red bell pepper, chopped

¼ cup fresh lime juice

3 tbsp olive oil

1 tsp honey

½ small shallot, minced

1 garlic clove, crushed

¼ tsp salt

Preparation:

Combine the lime juice with honey. Mix well with a fork. Slowly add the olive oil, whisking constantly. Now add the minced shallot, crushed garlic clove, and salt. Set aside.

Rinse the tomatoes and remove the stems. Cut into bite-sized pieces and set aside.

Cut the bell pepper lengthwise in half. Remove the stem and seeds. Cut into bite-sized pieces and set aside.

Now, in a large salad bowl, combine onion, green beans, cherry tomatoes, and bell pepper. Drizzle with previously prepared dressing and toss to combine.

Serve immediately.

Nutritional information per serving: Kcal: 268, Protein: 3.2g, Carbs: 20.5g, Fats: 21.6g

14. Lentil Salad

Ingredients:

1 cup lentils, cooked

1 medium-sized red bell pepper

½ cup sweet corn, drained

A handful of purple cabbage, shredded

A handful of lettuce, shredded

½ tsp salt

¼ tsp black pepper, freshly ground

2 tbsp olive oil

1 tbsp sesame seeds

Preparation:

First you have to cook your lentils. Use 3 cups of water for 1 cup of dry lentils. Cooked lentils will double in size. Bring the water to a boiling point, reduce the heat to medium and cover. Cook for about 15-20 minutes. Remove from the heat and drain. Transfer to a bowl and set aside.

Wash the pepper and cut lengthwise in half. Remove the stem and seeds. Chop into small pieces and set aside.

In a large colander, combine purple cabbage and lettuce. Rinse under running water and drain. Shred into tiny strips and set aside.

In a small mixing bowl, combine olive oil, sesame seeds, salt, and pepper. Mix until combined and set aside.

In a large salad bowl, combine cooked lentils, bell pepper, corn, cabbage, and lettuce. Drizzle with previously prepared dressing and toss to combine.

Serve immediately.

Nutritional information per serving: Kcal: 367, Protein: 18.7g, Carbs: 49g, Fats: 12g

15. Green Bean Salad

Ingredients:

1 lb fresh green beans

¼ cup extra virgin olive oil

2 garlic cloves, crushed

1 tbsp lime juice

Preparation:

Pour 4 cups of water in a deep pot. Bring to a boil over medium-high heat. Add beans and sprinkle with some salt. Cook for 5 minutes, or until tender. Remove from the heat and drain well. Transfer to a large bowl and let it chill for a while.

In a small mixing bowl, combine olive oil, garlic, and lime juice. Mix until well combined.

Drizzle the dressing over the beans and toss to coat well. Optionally, add a few lemon slices and finely chopped parsley for decoration before serving.

Enjoy!

Nutritional information per serving: Kcal: 296, Protein: 4.4g, Carbs: 19g, Fats: 25.5g

16. Raspberry Salad with Pumpkin Seeds

Ingredients:

1 tbsp pumpkin seeds

2 cups fresh raspberries

¼ tsp fresh rosemary, finely chopped

2 tbsp fresh lime juice

1 tsp cumin powder

1 tsp agave syrup

1 cup lettuce, chopped

Preparation:

Place the raspberries in a large colander and rinse under running water. Drain and set aside.

Rinse the lettuce under running water and drain. Chop into small pieces and set aside.

In a small mixing bowl, combine lime juice, cumin powder, and agave syrup. Mix until well combined.

In a large salad bowl, combine lettuce and raspberries. Drizzle with previously prepared dressing and toss to combine.

Refrigerate for 20 minutes before serving.

Nutritional information per serving: Kcal: 234, Protein: 6.1g, Carbs: 46.7g, Fats: 6.2g

17. Broccoli Salad with Tomatoes

Ingredients:

2 cups broccoli, halved

2 large tomatoes, chopped

2 tbsp olive oil

1 tbsp dried parsley, ground

¼ tsp Italian seasoning

Salt and pepper to taste

1 tbsp lemon juice, freshly squeezed

Preparation:

In a small bowl, combine olive oil, dried parsley, Italian seasoning, salt, pepper, and lemon juice. Mix until well combined and set aside.

Rinse the broccoli and cut each in half. Set aside.

Pour 3 cups of water in a deep pot. Bring to a boil over medium-high heat. Add broccoli and cook for 20 minutes, or until tender. Remove from the heat and drain. Set aside to chill for a while.

Wash the tomatoes and remove the stems. Chop into small

pieces and set aside.

In a large salad bowl, combine broccoli and tomatoes. Drizzle with previously prepared dressing and toss to combine.

Serve immediately.

Nutritional information per serving: Kcal: 188, Protein: 4.3g, Carbs: 13.5g, Fats: 14.9g

18. Seafood Salad

Ingredients:

1 small pack frozen mixed seafood

1 tbsp olive oil

1 small onion

1 cup cherry tomatoes

1 tsp chopped, dry rosemary

1 tbsp sweet corn

¼ tsp salt

1 tbsp freshly squeezed lemon juice

Preparation:

Preheat the olive oil in a saucepan over medium-high heat. Add seafood mix and cook for 10 minutes, crumbling the frozen mixture with a wooden spoon. Carefully add ¼ cup of water and continue to cook for 5 more minutes. Remove from the heat and allow it to cool.

Meanwhile prepare the remaining ingredients.

In a small mixing bowl, combine lemon juice, salt, and rosemary. Mix until combined and set aside.

Rinse the tomatoes under running water and remove the stems. Chop into small pieces and set aside.

In a large salad bowl, combine seafood mix, onion, and cherry tomatoes. Drizzle with previously prepared dressing and toss to combine.

Serve immediately.

Nutritional information per serving: Kcal: 208, Protein: 11.7g, Carbs: 22.7g, Fats: 8.7g

19. Dandelion Greens Salad

Ingredients:

2 cups fresh dandelion greens, roughly chopped

1 Roma tomato, finely chopped

½ cup fresh lemon juice

1 tbsp yellow mustard

Sea salt to taste

Preparation:

Place the dandelion greens in a large colander and rinse under running water. Drain and chop into small pieces. Set aside.

Wash the tomato and remove the stem. Cut into bite-sized pieces and set aside.

In a small mixing bowl, combine lemon juice, yellow mustard, and sea salt. Mix until salt has been disolved.

Now, place the greens in a salad bowl and drizzle with previously prepared dressing. Toss to combine and serve immediately.

Instead of dandelion greens, feel free to use baby arugula,

baby spinach, or some other leafy green vegetable.

Nutritional information per serving: Kcal: 90, Protein: 4.7g, Carbs: 13.9g, Fats: 2.4g

20. Veal Salad with Fresh Veggies

Ingredients:

1 lb veal cutlets

1 large tomato

1 large green bell pepper

½ cup cabbage, grated

2 tbsp olive oil

¼ tsp dried thyme, ground

¼ tsp dried parsley, ground

1 garlic clove, minced

Salt and pepper to taste

Preparation:

Rinse the meat under running water and pat dry with a kitchen paper. Transfer to a cutting board and cut into thin strips. Generously rub with salt, pepper, thyme, parsley, and olive oil. Set aside for 10 minutes.

Meanwhile, preheat the grill to medium-high. Grill for 3-5 minutes on each side. Remove from the heat and set aside to chill for a while.

Prepare the remaining vegetables.

Cut the pepper lengthwise in half. Remove the stem and seeds. Chop into thin strips and set aside.

Wash the tomato and remove the stem. Chop into small pieces and set aside.

Now, combine bell pepper, tomato, and cabbage in a salad bowl. Top with meat and sprinkle with some more salt and olive oil.

Nutritional information per serving: Kcal: 343, Protein: 35g, Carbs: 4.9g, Fats: 20.1g

21. Grilled Chicken Salad

Ingredients:

2 pieces chicken breast, boneless and skinless

¼ cup silken tofu, sliced

1 cup lamb's lettuce

1 cup cherry tomatoes

1 small zucchini, chopped

¼ tsp of red pepper, ground

2 tbsp olive oil

¼ tsp salt

Preparation:

Wash and pat dry the meat with some kitchen paper. Transfer to a cutting board and cut into bite-sized pieces. Brush with some salt and olive oil and set aside.

Peel and chop the zucchini into thin slices. Sprinkle with some salt and set aside.

Preheat the grill to a medium-high heat. Add chicken and zucchini. Grill the chicken 2-3 minutes per side. Grill the zucchini 1-2 minutes per side.

Now, grill tofu for 2 minutes per side.

Rinse the lamb's lettuce using a large colander. Drain and transfer to a large bowl. Add cherry tomatoes, tofu, zucchini, and red pepper. Mix all well and top with chicken.

Serve immediately.

Nutritional information per serving: Kcal: 286, Protein: 26.2g, Carbs: 7g, Fats: 17.4g

22. Lettuce Salad with Walnuts

Ingredients:

2 cups Iceberg lettuce, chopped

1 large orange, peeled and wedged

2 tbsp walnuts, roughly chopped

¼ cup dates, pitted and finely chopped

1 tbsp fresh lemon juice

1 tbsp olive oil

¼ tsp dried thyme, ground

Preparation:

Place the lettuce in a large colander. Rinse under running water and drain. Chop into small pieces and place in a large bowl. Set aside.

Peel the orange and divide into wedges. Cut each wedge in half and add to the bowl with lettuce.

In a small mixing bowl, combine lemon juice, olive oil, and thyme. Mix until well combined and drizzle over the salad.

Finally top with dates and walnuts.

Serve immediately.

Nutritional information per serving: Kcal: 224, Protein: 3.6g, Carbs: 30.2g, Fats: 12g

23. Homemade Tuna Salad

Ingredients:

1 (12oz) tuna steak

¼ cup spring onions, chopped

2 tbsp extra-virgin olive oil

¼ tsp sea salt

¼ tsp chili pepper

1/8 tsp white pepper, ground

1 tbsp fresh lemon juice

Preparation:

Rinse the tuna steak under running water and pat-dry with a kitchen towel. Generously rub with salt, pepper, and olive oil. Set aside.

Meanwhile, preheat the grill to medium-high heat. Cook for 4-5 minutes on each side. Remove from the grill and set aside to chill for a while.

Using two forks, flake the tuna into thin strips. Transfer to a salad bowl, and add spring onions. Add the remaining olive oil and sprinkle with some salt.

Finally, drizzle with lemon juice and serve immediately.

Enjoy!

Nutritional information per serving: Kcal: 293, Protein: 34.1g, Carbs: 0.8g, Fats: 16.5g

24. Lettuce and Tomato Salad

Ingredients:

2 cups cherry tomatoes, roughly chopped

2 cups Iceberg lettuce, finely chopped

1 tsp apple cider vinegar

¼ tsp of sea salt

¼ tsp red pepper flakes

½ tbsp extra virgin olive oil

Preparation:

Rinse the cherry tomatoes and remove the stems. Roughly chop it into bite-sized pieces and set aside.

Using a large colander, rinse the lettuce thoroughly under running water. Drain and chop into small pieces. Set aside.

In a small mixing bowl, combine apple cider vinegar, sea salt, red pepper, and olive oil. Mix until combined and set aside.

Now, in a large salad bowl, combine cherry tomatoes and lettuce. Drizzle with previously prepared dressing and toss to combine.

Serve immediately.

Nutritional information per serving: Kcal: 142, Protein: 3.7g, Carbs: 17.6g, Fats: 8g

25. Creamy Chicken Salad

Ingredients:

4 oz chicken breast, skinless and boneless

1 cup Romaine lettuce, chopped

1 medium onion, peeled and sliced

5 cherry tomatoes, chopped

2 tbsp low-fat cream

1 tsp fresh parsley, finely chopped

1 tbsp extra-virgin olive oil

¼ tsp chili powder

1 tbsp lemon juice

Salt and pepper

Preparation:

Rinse the chicken under running water and pat-dry with a kitchen paper. Transfer to a cutting board and cut into thin slices. Using your hands, rub with some salt and pepper. Set aside.

In a small saucepan, combine cream, parsley, chili powder,

and a pinch of salt and pepper. Heat up over medium-high heat. Bring it to a boil and remove from the heat. Give it a good stir and set aside.

Preheat the grill to medium-high heat. Add chicken and cook for 3 minutes on each side. Remove from the grill and set aside.

Wash and prepare the remaining vegetables.

In a large salad bowl, combine lettuce, onion, and tomatoes. Top with chicken and drizzle all with cream sauce. Mix until well coated and serve immediately.

Enjoy!

Nutritional information per serving: Kcal: 223, Protein: 17.7g, Carbs: 19.2g, Fats: 9.5g

26. Leafy Greens Salad with Orange Dressing

Ingredients:

2 cups Iceberg lettuce, roughly chopped

1 cup baby spinach, roughly chopped

½ cup Mozzarella cheese, sliced

2 tbsp orange juice, freshly squeezed

1 tsp apple cider vinegar

½ tsp Italian seasoning

¼ tsp black pepper, ground

¼ tsp salt

Preparation:

In a large colander, combine lettuce and spinach. Rinse under running water and drain. Chop into bite-sized pieces and transfer to a large salad bowl. Set aside.

In a small mixing bowl, combine orange juice, apple cider vinegar, Italian seasoning, black pepper, and salt. Mix until well combined.

Cut the cheese into thin slices and add to the salad. Drizzle all with previously prepared dressing and toss to combine.

Optionally, add a few olives for some extra flavor.

Enjoy!

Nutritional information per serving: Kcal: 85, Protein: 5.6g, Carbs: 8.8g, Fats: 3.6g

27. Radicchio Salad

Ingredients:

1 large radish, roughly chopped

1 large cucumber, sliced

¼ cup lemon juice, freshly squeezed

1 tbsp fresh parsley, finely chopped

¼ tsp black pepper, ground

¼ tsp salt

1 tsp yellow mustard

Preparation:

In a small mixing bowl, combine lemon juice, parsley, pepper, salt, and mustard. Mix untill smooth and set aside.

Wash the radish and trim off the outer leaves. Transfer to a cutting board and chop into small pieces. Place in a large salad bowl and set aside.

Wash the cucumber and cut into thin slices.

Combine cucumber with the radish and drizzle all with the previously prepared dressing. Toss to combine and serve immediately.

Enjoy!

Nutritional information per serving: Kcal: 67, Protein: 2.9g, Carbs: 13.4g, Fats: 1.1g

28. Steamed Spinach Salad

Ingredients:

4 oz fresh spinach, chopped

1 tsp apple cider vinegar

1 tbsp extra-virgin olive oil

¼ tsp salt

¼ tsp Italian seasoning

¼ tsp black pepper, ground

Preparation:

Using a large colander, rinse the spinach under cold running water. Drain and chop into small pieces.

In a small mixing bowl, combine apple cider vinegar, olive oil, salt, Italian seasoning, and pepper. Mix until combined and set aside.

Pour 1 cup of water in a deep pot. Bring to a boil over medium-high heat. Place the spinach in a steam basket. Place the basket on top of the pot and cook for 5 minutes, or until wilted. Remove from the heat and transfer to a serving dish.

Drizzle with previously prepared dressing and serve immediately.

Enjoy!

Nutritional information per serving: Kcal: 152, Protein: 3.3g, Carbs: 4.6g, Fats: 14.8g

29. Red Cabbage Tomato Salad

Ingredients:

2 cups fresh cabbage, thinly shredded

½ cup plum tomatoes, chopped

¼ cup apple cider vinegar

¼ tsp dried thyme, ground

¼ tsp dried oregano, ground

2 tbsp olive oil

Salt and pepper

Preparation:

In a small mixing bowl, combine apple cider vinegar, dried thyme, dried oregano, olive oil, salt, and pepper. Mix until combined and set aside.

Rinse the cabbage under running water. Transfer to a cutting board and shred into thin strips. Transfer to a large bowl and set aside.

Rinse the tomatoes and remove the stems. Chop into bite-sized pieces and add to the bowl with cabbage.

Drizzle all with previously prepared dressing and serve

immediately

Enjoy!

Nutritional information per serving: Kcal: 155, Protein: 1.5g, Carbs: 6.9g, Fats: 14.2g

30. Turkey Pepper Salad

Ingredients:

4 oz turkey breast, skinless and boneless

1 large red bell pepper, chopped

1 large yellow bell pepper, chopped

1 cucumber, chunked

1 small purple onion, diced

1 tbsp olive oil

1 tbsp white wine vinegar

½ tsp dried thyme, ground

¼ tsp dried rosemary, ground

2 tbsp lime juice, freshly squeezed

Salt and pepper

Preparation:

Rinse the meat under running water and pat-dry with a kitchen towel. Transfer to a cutting board and cut into thin slices.

Place the meat in a deep pot and add water enough to

cover. Bring to a boil over medium-high heat. Cook for 10-15 minutes, or until fork-tender. Remove from the heat and set aside. Optionally, place on a grill for 2 minutes on each side to get nicely golden brown color.

In a small mixing bowl, combine olive oil, white wine vinegar, dried thyme, dried rosemary, lime juice, salt, and pepper. Mix until well combined and set aside.

Wash and prepare the remaining ingredients.

In a large salad bowl, combine bell pepper, cucumber, and onion. Top with turkey slices and drizzle all with previously prepared dressing.

Serve immediately.

Nutritional information per serving: Kcal: 206, Protein: 12.5g, Carbs: 24.1g, Fats: 8.5g

31. Spinach Egg Salad

Ingredients:

2 cups fresh spinach, chopped

1 large egg, hard-boiled

1 small onion, sliced

¼ cup ricotta cheese, crumbled

1 small cucumber, sliced

1 tsp balsamic vinegar

1 tbsp olive oil

2 garlic cloves, crushed

¼ tsp smoked paprika

Salt and pepper

Preparation:

Place the egg in a deep pot and add enough water to cover. Bring to a boil over medium-high heat. Cook for 10-12 minutes. Remove from the heat and transfer to the prepared ice cold water bath. Let it sit for 5 minutes to chill.

Meanwhile, rinse the spinach under running water and

drain. Chop into small pieces and set aside.

Pour 1 cup of water in a deep pot. Bring to a boil over medium-high heat. Place the spinach in a steam basket. Place the basket on top of the pot and steam for 3-5 minutes, or until wilted. Remove from the heat and transfer to a large salad bowl.

In a small mixing bowl, combine balsamic vinegar, olive oil, garlic, smoked paprika, salt, and pepper. Mix until well combined.

Peel the egg and cut into thin wedges. Add to the bowl with spinach, along with onion and cucumber. Drizzle all with previously prepared dressing and top with ricotta cheese.

Serve cold.

Nutritional information per serving: Kcal: 188, Protein: 9.1g, Carbs: 12.8g, Fats: 12.3g

32. Roasted Beet Salad with Walnuts

Ingredients:

1 large beet, sliced

2 cups fresh arugula, chopped

¼ cup goat's cheese, crumbled

½ ripe avocado, sliced

1 tbsp olive oil

1 tbsp red wine vinegar

2 tbsp walnuts, roughly chopped

Salt and pepper

Preparation:

Preheat the grill to medium-high heat.

Wash the beets and trim off the green parts. Cut into thin slices and brush with some olive oil. Sprinkle with some salt and pepper.

Grill the beets for 4-5 minutes on each side. Remove to a plate and set aside.

Rinse the arugula under running water. Drain and torn into

small pieces. Place in a large salad bowl and set aside.

In a small mixing bowl, combine olive oil, red wine vinegar, salt, and pepper. Mix until combined and set aside.

Now, combine arugula, beets, avocado, and goat's cheese in a bowl. Mix until combined and then drizzle with previously prepared dressing. Toss to combine and top with walnuts before serving.

Enjoy!

Nutritional information per serving: Kcal: 228, Protein: 6.9g, Carbs: 7.8g, Fats: 20.1g

33. Avocado Salad with Pickled Onions

Ingredients:

1 ripe avocado, sliced

¼ cup black beans, cooked

1 medium-sized purple onion, sliced

2 tbsp fresh parsley, finely chopped

2 tbsp balsamic vinegar

1 tsp coconut syrup

½ cup cherry tomatoes

¼ tsp cumin powder

1 whole lime, juiced

1 tbsp olive oil

Salt and pepper

Preparation:

Peel the onion and cut into thin slices. Place in a small bowl and drizzle with balsamic vinegar, coconut syrup, and some salt. Let it marinate for 15 minutes. Stir occasionally.

Cut the avocado lengthwise in half. Peel and remove the

pit. Cut into bite-sized pieces and set aside.

In a large salad bowl, combine avocado, beans, parsley, and pickled onions. Add the remaining marinade from the onions. Sprinkle all with cumin powder and lime juice. Add a pinch of salt and pepper and give it a good stir.

Serve immediately.

Nutritional information per serving: Kcal: 265, Protein: 5.6g, Carbs: 23.3g, Fats: 18.1g

34. Quinoa Salad with Spicy Vinaigrette

Ingredients:

½ cup quinoa

1 small cucumber, sliced

1 cup cherry tomatoes, chopped

¼ cup Feta cheese, crumbled

2 tbsp olive oil

1 tbsp red wine vinegar

1 garlic clove, minced

½ tsp red pepper flakes

¼ tsp smoked paprika

¼ tsp dried oregano, ground

Salt and pepper

Preparation:

Place the quinoa in a medium saucepan and add 1 cup of water. Bring to a boil over medium-high heat. Cook for 12-15 minutes, or until all the liquid has been soaked up and evaporated. Remove from the heat and fluff with a wooden spoon. Set aside.

In a small mixing bowl, combine olive oil, red wine vinegar, garlic, red pepper flakes, smoked paprika, dried oregano, salt, and pepper. Mix until well combined and set aside.

Wash and prepare the remaining ingredients.

In a large salad bowl, combine cooked quinoa, cucumber, cherry tomatoes, and feta cheese. Drizzle all with previously prepared dressing and give it a good stir.

Optionally, drizzle with some fresh lemo juice.

Enjoy!

Nutritional information per serving: Kcal: 186, Protein: 5.3g, Carbs: 19g, Fats: 10.5g

35. Greek Salad with Kalamata Olives

Ingredients:

1 cup grape tomatoes, halved

1 large cucumber, sliced

1 small purple onion, sliced

¼ cup Feta cheese, crumbled

¼ cup Kalamata olives, pitted and sliced

1 tbsp balsamic vinegar

2 tbsp olive oil

1 whole lemon, juiced

½ tsp dried oregano, ground

¼ tsp dried rosemary, ground

1 tbsp fresh parsley, finely chopped

½ tsp black pepper, freshly ground

½ tsp kosher salt

Preparation:

Rinse the tomatoes under running water. Cut each in half

and place in a large salad bowl. Set aside.

Wash the cucumber and lengthwise in half. Cut into thin slices and add to the bowl.

Peel the onion and cut into small pieces. Add to the bowl with the remaining ingredients.

In a small mixing bowl, combine balsamic vinegar, olive oil, lemon juice, dried oregano, dried rosemary, parsley, black pepper, and salt. Mix until combined and set aside.

Now, add cheese and olives to the remaining ingredients and drizzle all with previously prepared dressing. Toss to combine and serve immediately.

Enjoy!

Nutritional information per serving: Kcal: 247, Protein: 5.1g, Carbs: 14.9g, Fats: 20.3g

36. Balsamic Steak Salad with Peaches

Ingredients:

4 oz lean skirt steak, thinly sliced

1 large peach, wedged

2 cups fresh arugula, chopped

¼ cup blue cheese, crumbled

¼ cup balsamic vinegar

1 garlic clove, crushed

1 tbsp olive oil

1 whole lime, freshly squeezed

Salt and pepper

Preparation:

Rinse well the meat and pat-dry with a kitchen towel. Transfer to a cutting board and cut into thin slices. Place in a deep bowl and add balsamic vinegar, garlic, salt, and pepper. Let it marinate for 20 minutes.

Meanwhile, preheat the grill to medium-high heat. Grill the steak for 3-5 minutes on each side.

Rinse the arugula thoroughly under running water. Drain and chop into small pieces. Set aside.

In a small mixing bowl, combine olive oil, lime juice, salt, and pepper. Mix until combined and set aside.

In a large mixing bowl, combine arugula, blue cheese, and peach. Top with steaks and sprinkle with previously prepared dressing.

Toss to combine and serve immediately.

Nutritional information per serving: Kcal: 193, Protein: 13.5g, Carbs: 8.3g, Fats: 12g

37. Chickpea Salad with Wild Garlic

Ingredients:

1 cup canned chickpeas, drained and rinsed

1 small red bell pepper, chopped

1 small cucumber, chopped

½ cup spring onions, chopped

¼ cup wild garlic, finely chopped

¼ cup cottage cheese, crumbled

2 tbsp olive oil

1 tbsp apple cider vinegar

2 tbsp lemon juice, freshly squeezed

1 tbsp fresh parsley, finely chopped

¼ tsp red pepper flakes

Salt and pepper

Preparation:

Place the chickpeas in a colander and rinse well. Drain and set aside.

Cut the bell pepper lengthwise in half. Remove the stem and seeds. Chop into small pieces and set aside.

Wash the cucumber and cut into thin slices. Set aside.

Rinse the wild garlic leaves under running water. Torn into small pieces and set aside.

In a small mixing bowl, combine olive oil, apple cider vinegar, lemon juice, parsley, salt, and pepper. Mix until combined and set aside.

In a large salad bowl, combine chickpeas, red bell pepper, cucumber, spring onions, wild garlic, and cottage cheese. Drizzle with previously prepared dressing and toss to combine.

Serve immediately.

Nutritional information per serving: Kcal: 230, Protein: 8.1g, Carbs: 27.1g, Fats: 11g

38. Spinach Pecorino Salad

Ingredients:

2 cups baby spinach, chopped

¼ cup Pecorino cheese, grated

1 medium-sized Granny Smith's apple, cored and chopped

2 tbsp lemon juice, freshly squeezed

1 tbsp balsamic vinegar

1 tsp lime zest, freshly grated

Salt and pepper

Preparation:

Place the spinach in a large colander and rinse under running water. Drain and chop into small pieces. Set aside.

Wash the apple and cut in half. Remove the core and cut into thin slices. Set aside.

In a small mixing bowl, combine lemon juice, balsamic vinegar, lime zest, salt, and pepper. Mix until combined and set aside.

In a large salad bowl, combine baby spinach, Pecorino cheese, and apple. Drizzle with previously prepared dressing and toss to combine.

Optionally, sprinkle with some pomegranate seeds before serving.

Enjoy!

Nutritional information per serving: Kcal: 205, Protein: 10g, Carbs: 25.3g, Fats: 8.5g

39. Chicken Salad with Pecans

Ingredients:

4 oz chicken breast, skinless and boneless

½ cup grapes

¼ cup spring onions, chopped

1 cup Romaine lettuce, chopped

2 tbsp pecans, roughly chopped

¼ cup Greek yogurt

2 tbsp lemon juice, freshly squeezed

1 tsp Dijon mustard

1 tbsp fresh dill, finely chopped

1 tbsp fresh parsley, finely chopped

¼ tsp smoked paprika

Salt and pepper

Preparation:

Preheat the grill to medium-high heat.

In a mixing bowl, combine Greek yogurt, lemon juice, Dijon

mustard, dill, parsley, smoked paprika, salt, and pepper. Mix until combined and set aside.

Rinse the chicken and pat-dry with a kitchen towel. Sprinkle with some salt and pepper and grill for 3 minutes on each side.

Now, place chicken in a deep bowl along with grapes and pecans. Drizzle with yogurt mixture and mix until all well coated

Serve immediately.

Nutritional information per serving: Kcal: 201, Protein: 11.4g, Carbs: 7.8g, Fats: 14.7g

40. Green Bean Fusilli Salad

Ingredients:

4 oz. fusilli pasta

1 cup green beans

¼ cup Feta cheese, crumbled

¼ cup olives, pitted and chopped

2 garlic cloves, minced

½ onion, finely chopped

1 cup yogurt, low-fat

1 tsp. yellow mustard

2 tbsp. olive oil

½ tsp. dried dill, ground

½ tsp. red pepper, ground

Salt

Preparation:

Place the pasta in a deep pot. Add enough water to cover and bring it to a boil. Sprinkle with some salt and cook for 10 minutes over medium-high heat. Remove from the heat and transfer to a large colander. Rinse under cold running water and set aside. Place the green beans in a deep pot and cover with water. Bring to a boil over medium-high heat and cook for 5 minutes. Remove from the heat and drain. Set aside. Preheat one tablespoon of olive oil in a large skillet over medium-high heat. Add onions and garlic. Stir-fry for 2-3 minutes, or until translucent. Add green beans and cook for 5 minutes. Remove from the heat and transfer to a large salad bowl.

Add pasta to the bowl and stir well. Set aside.

Now, combine the remaining olive oil, yogurt, mustard, dried dill, red pepper, and a pinch of salt in a mixing bowl. Mix until well combined and pour over prepared beans and pasta. Top with olives and cheese before serving.

Nutritional information per serving: Kcal: 264, Protein: 9.3g, Carbs: 31.5g, Fats: 11.2g

41. Cooked Celery Salad

Ingredients:

4 celery sticks, with leaves

1 whole lemon, juiced

3 tbsp. walnuts, halved

1 small purple onion, finely chopped

2 tbsp. white wine vinegar

2 cups lamb's lettuce, roughly chopped

1 tsp. flaxseed oil

½ tsp. salt

½ tsp. black pepper, ground

Preparation:

Rinse the celery under cold running water and drain. Transfer to a cutting board and separate sticks and leaves. Chop the sticks into strips and finely chop the leaves. Set aside.

Transfer the celery sticks in a deep pot. Cover with water and bring to a boil over medium-high heat. Cook for 8 minutes. Add celery leaves and fresh lemon juice. Stir once and cook for 2-3 minutes more. Remove from the heat and drain. Rinse all under cold running water immediately. Set aside.

In a mixing bowl, combine onions, vinegar, salt, and pepper. Mix until well incorporated. Add flaxseed oil and mix again until combined.

Now, arrange the lamb's lettuce over a serving dish and top with celery. Drizzle with previously prepared dressing.

Serve cold.

Nutritional information per serving: Kcal: 273, Protein: 8.8g, Carbs: 17.9g, Fats: 19g

42. Avocado Egg Salad

Ingredients:

1 ripe avocado, cut into cubes

2 large eggs, hard-boiled

2 spring onions, chopped

½ cup Greek yogurt

1 tbsp. sour cream

1 whole lime, juiced

1 tsp. fresh thyme, finely chopped

Salt and pepper to taste

Preparation:

Place the eggs in a deep pot. Add water enough to cover and bring to a boil over medium-high heat. Cook for 10-12 minutes. Remove from the heat and transfer to a bowl with ice cold water. You can add a few ice cubes to speed up the process. Peel and cut into bite-sized pieces. Set aside.

Peel the avocado and cut lengthwise in half. Remove the pit and cut into bite-sized cubes. Set aside.

In a mixing bowl, combine Greek yogurt, sour cream, lime

juice, thyme, salt, and pepper. Mix until combined.

In a serving bowl, combine eggs and avocado. Drizzle with previously prepared dressing and give it a good stir.

Serve immediately.

Nutritional information per serving: Kcal: 343, Protein: 14g, Carbs: 16.3g, Fats: 27g

43. Grilled Mustard Turkey Salad

Ingredients:

8 oz. turkey breast, skinless and boneless

1 tbsp. yellow mustard

3 tsp. olive oil

½ tsp. salt

½ tsp. black pepper, ground

2 cups Romaine lettuce, chopped

1 cup lamb's lettuce

½ cup cherry tomatoes, chopped

1 tbsp. Parmesan cheese, shredded

2 tsp. red wine vinegar

Preparation:

Rinse and drain the turkey breast. Transfer to a cutting board and cut into thin slices. Set aside.

In a small mixing bowl, combine 2 teaspoons of olive oil, salt, black pepper, and mustard. Mix until combined and pour over the meat. Rub with your hands to allow flavors to penetrate into the meat. Cover the dish with a plastic foil and refrigerate for 1 hour.

Preheat the grill to medium-high. Add meat and grill for 3-4 minutes on each side. Remove from the heat and transfer to a cutting board. Let it chill for a while and then cut into strips.

Wash and prepare the vegetables.

In a large salad bowl, combine lettuce, lamb's lettuce, and cherry tomatoes. Top with turkey strips and drizzle with red wine vinegar. Sprinkle with parmesan cheese and serve immediately.

Nutritional information per serving: Kcal: 248, Protein: 25g, Carbs: 9.6g, Fats: 12.4g

44. Shrimp Avocado Salad

Ingredients:

4 oz. shrimps, cleaned and deveined

½ ripe avocado, chopped

¼ cup Feta cheese, crumbled

1 medium-sized green bell pepper, chopped

½ cup cherry tomatoes, chopped

½ cup fresh mint, roughly chopped

1 small purple onion, chopped

¼ cup green olives, pitted

1 tbsp. fresh parsley, finely chopped

1 whole lime, juiced

¼ tsp. garlic powder

¼ tsp. dried oregano, ground

½ tsp. red pepper flakes

2 tbsp. olive oil

Salt to taste

Preparation:

In a small mixing bowl, combine lime juice, oregano, garlic, 1 tablespoon of olive oil, pepper flakes, and salt. Mix until well combined and set aside.

Wash and prepare the vegetables.

In a large salad bowl, combine cherry tomatoes, mint, purple onion, green olives, and parsley. Drizzle with previously prepared dressing and refrigerate for 20 minutes.

Preheat the remaining oil in a skillet over medium-high heat. Add shrimps and sprinkle with some salt and red pepper. Cook for 2-3 minutes, or until set. Remove from the heat and set aside to chill for a while.

Now, add cheese and avocado to the salad. Mix again and top with shrimps. Garnish with fresh mint and serve immediately.

Nutritional information per serving: Kcal: 264, Protein: 12.6g, Carbs: 12.2g, Fats: 19.6g

ADDITIONAL TITLES FROM THIS AUTHOR

70 Effective Meal Recipes to Prevent and Solve Being Overweight: Burn Fat Fast by Using Proper Dieting and Smart Nutrition

By

Joe Correa CSN

48 Acne Solving Meal Recipes: The Fast and Natural Path to Fixing Your Acne Problems in Less Than 10 Days!

By

Joe Correa CSN

41 Alzheimer's Preventing Meal Recipes: Reduce or Eliminate Your Alzheimer's Condition in 30 Days or Less!

By

Joe Correa CSN

70 Effective Breast Cancer Meal Recipes: Prevent and Fight Breast Cancer with Smart Nutrition and Powerful Foods

By

Joe Correa CSN

www.ingramcontent.com/pod-product-compliance
Lightning Source LLC
Chambersburg PA
CBHW052030070526
44584CB00016B/1985